AUTOPSY

AUTOPSY

POEMS BY
Donte Collins

—

button
poetry

Published by Button Poetry / Exploding Pinecone Press
Minneapolis, MN 55403 | http://www.buttonpoetry.com

—

Cover Design: Nikki Clark

Author Photograph: Marlen Boro

ISBN 978-1-943735-11-2

Every word is for my late mother Mary Lou Collins
& anyone who has ever helped us carry
in the groceries

The most beautiful part of your body is
where it's headed.

– OCEAN VUONG, "SOMEDAY I'LL LOVE OCEAN VUONG"

...And my family go through it with me
We lost a lot, all I feel is empty.

– LAMAR COLLINS, FACEBOOK

If you aren't able to describe it, you will
not be able to survive it.

– JAMES BALDWIN, THE CROSS OF REDEMPTION:
UNCOLLECTED WRITINGS

DEATH AIN'T NOTHIN' BUT A SONG

my mother moved out
of her body   decided it
was no longer worthy

> it couldn't contain her laughter
> she couldn't obey the house
> rules of human   her spirit

that young & fresh fever   wanted
to call the night her dance club
wanted to try on new clothes
stay out later

> my mother now wears the world
> dresses herself with the tall grass
> blushes her cheeks with red clay

she laughs & a forest fire awakens
she laughs & every mountain bows
to her sharp thunder   she laughs

> & each cicada begins to sing   last
> night Saint Paul was cloaked in steam:
> *fog traveled from some distant heat*

no, i think   you've got it all wrong
someone must have asked my mother

to dance

CONTENTS

Death Ain't Nothin' but a Song

3 Don't Tell Your Uber Driver You're Going to an Orgy

6 Sonnet on Sweet

9 [Definitions]

11 Other Things They Would Have Found

12 The Orphan Performs an Autopsy on the Garden

14 Thirteen Ways of Looking at Thirteen

20 Grief: The Inconvenient Translator

21 Old Rondo - Age 16

23 What the Dead Know by Heart

24 The Orphan Performs an Autopsy on Old Rondo

25 Whiteness Shops for a Prayer

26 The Orphan Performs an Autopsy on the National Anthem

27 New Country

29 The Orphan Dines with Ghosts

31 In Which the Orphan's Sister Is Murdered Six Months after His Mother's Death

32 Five Stages of Grief

35 Grief, Again

36 Teething: A Crumbling Pantoum

37 Alphabet Soup

39 The Orphan Performs an Autopsy on Adoption

41 Alternate Beginning: The Game

43 Adoption Day: Homecoming, 1998

45 To Keep from Saying Orphan

47 Grief Sestina

49 Long Story Short

51 *Acknowledgments*

53 *About the Author*

DON'T TELL YOUR UBER DRIVER
YOU'RE GOING TO AN ORGY

besides, her name is diane & she only has this job
because her niece says she should be more *social*

do not, nervously, try to cover up your mistake by
saying you meant *b-oar-d mee-tin-g*. besides, it's
3 a.m. & the only things open this late

can
also
                                            request
                                            another
                                            thing
to
open

do not try to cancel the ride. it is not your account. those who
sent for your body were kind enough to pay the $15.50 it took
for you to arrive. your nails are already too jagged to chew on

you've produced enough sweat to fill the vehicle & drown
you both. you consider headphones. you consider ripping out
your tongue in fear of confessing more & before you reach for
the handle to tuck & roll clean out of her 2004 Honda Civic
she says:
                                                    how many

                    bodies will you try on tonight / & suddenly she is your mother
                                                    or her ghost
                    & suddenly your blood stiffens / retreats / rewinds / no one died
                                                    the casket
                    is still just wood / unchopped / reassembled / the tree, resurrected
                                                    working &
                    grief is not yet a garden of thorns blooming

in your chest
& grief is not yet a question you've answered with sex
the slow
teasing out of sweat like loose thread unraveling
your sadness
& look: you're just a boy / grieving until he too is a thing
to grieve / until
his pulse is as thin & damp as an obituary panting beneath quaking

hands & what
is an orgy, if not the opposite
of a funeral, if not an attempt to

press your
pulse to as many strangers as possible: to compare
how alive
you still are. & isn't the car now your mother's hearse / parading
her body

to that freshly gutted plot of earth & suddenly you are the driver
/ suddenly
the sky breaks a sweat / its whole body blue & ballooning wet
but you're also the casket
but you're also the soggy grave parting its greedy
lips / you ghost
orphan / you motherless phantom considering the dive

following
your maker, buried alive / i know, you desire decay, donte

/ you desire
now, a way to die without losing your body: so why not use
it / why not let a stranger lick the grief from your palms & this too is eulogy
this too is prayer
& this too can water the seeds to conjure

thornless crops
can sing back alive whatever parts of you died

                                                                    with her
                              whatever leapt into your mother's closing crate

& diane slams the brakes. *you have arrived* she says *be safe*. his
apartment door: a pearly gate, a cliff overlooking a thrashing lake
& your blood begins & you lighthouse your tongue & you ship
wreck an entire room to driftwood. O this festival of lament

O this sloppy surgery, this homemade baptism. you reek of grief
they taste the salt streaming your cheek. you lonely riot, you laughing
graveyard. you hungry & haunted boy. i know, i know. you want
so badly to feel alive. you want so badly to be born
                                                                    again

SONNET ON SWEET
after Tarell Alvin McCraney

back then they would have tied me to a post
gave the whip to the sweet boy i wrapped
my lips around until he wept the most
brackish prayer: *he dripped like maple sap*
each *tthh-wack* opens a small sky in my skin
he swings softly & avoids my old welts
lynch say *beat the slave out of the sin*
so massa take pride in my lover's help
can't produce slaves if men lay with men
can't run free when massa stole your feet
plantation can't afford no cotton gin
when two black bucks is worth a pound of meat
so massa rubbed sugar sap in my scars
& left me till my black swelled bright as stars

orphan [ˈôrfən/]

i.e. the lawyer says: you are not orphans as long as you have each other
i.e. like any good orphan, he took up gardening, attempts to forgive the
earth i.e. the orphan mothers his own origin

autopsy [ˈôˌtäpsē]

i.e. they would have found dandelion seeds had they done the autopsy:
they would have found a field of burning lavender had they cut her open

OTHER THINGS THEY WOULD HAVE FOUND

vineyard of charred candle wicks
fraying wicker broom
grocery bags of unopened letters
garage of rusting tap shoes
coffee-stained divorce papers
divorce papers stuffed in a shoebox
divorce papers framed on the wall
garden of swinging dandelions
basement brimming with box cutters
wedding ring singed beneath ash
wedding ring severed at the mouth
wedding ring bent into bobby pin
grocery bag of other rolled up grocery bags
an oak foot-powered sewing machine
two antique hair dryers
washboard & elbow grease
grocery bag of clean rags
forest of ripening plums
cupboard of chipped plates
collection of cast iron skillets
instructions on how to properly play sequence
rusted tin box spilling with recipes, receipts
court gavels: one for each child
ashtray of soot pennies
a badge & a bad hip
white flag stained red
two infant black girl hands,
extended: longing to be held

THE ORPHAN PERFORMS AN AUTOPSY ON THE GARDEN

there are many ways to pull a weed
but only one will keep the garden
clean come the end of summer

your mother will be dead
13 years - 2 months - 11 days - 7 hours from now

& you curse her beneath your breath. flick beaded sweat gathered
like pearls at the crease of your brow & continue to rip up the earth

why does heat make the body confess what it will not do otherwise?
drunk on july & nerve you rip handfuls of color from along the fence
thorns like brief alarms warning your fevered temper of what blood
will soon stain your teeth. never. ruin. your. mother's. new. plants

your mother will be dead
3 years - 6 months - 9 hours from now

& a man, not your father, calls you *baby*. calls the house phone past
midnight. waits, like warm fog, outside your bedroom window, wants
to use your mouth to raise his children. why does heat make the body
confess what it will not do otherwise?

sneaking out of a house built of creaking wood can only end with
red smeared across checkered linoleum. can only cause a mother to
lock the doors from the outside. deadbolt & *don't disrespect my house
again!* basement stairs & belt buckle branded—a birthmark across
your sprouting back. see me: a field of dry & rebellious wheat thrashing
until flaming. until ash

your mother will be dead
3 days - 6 hours - 14 minutes from now

& wants to take you to lunch. insists on giving you all your old inhalers,
face-cream, old shoes. says *you never know. says if i died i wouldn't
know what to do with all of this*—points—the china cabinet, a small

museum of memories. says *we laughed a lot, too.* our faces framed &
frozen to happy. says *if you & lamar don't know i love you, know now*
& now she is weeping. see her: a black sky cracking, offering water: as
if to say: forgiveness is a fertile thing—is what makes tomorrow grow

& / just / like / that / she's / dead / a / porch / light / gone / out / a
wind / chime / songless / sunken / into / soil / you / untethered / 19
returning / to / an / empty / home / find / your / hands / busy / in
an / abandoned / garden / joy / must / be / a / flower / among / all
of / this / knotted / agony / there / are / many / ways / to / pull / grief
from / the / body / but / only / one / will / keep / the / boy / alive

THIRTEEN WAYS OF LOOKING AT THIRTEEN
after Patricia Smith

they ask you to prove it: *describe its pink perfectly*
you are lying & looking down. you are thinking of
clever ways to creep out of the conversation. they
ask if you used a condom, you consider your op
tions. think it cool to say no because you're too raw for
that. too axe cologne & black muscle shirt, more shirt than
muscle. more mask than masculine. you say *soft, it felt*
good, went in, one hour & the games begin. how straight
can you pretend to be? what new sex story can you
steal from t.v. & wear like padded muscles. you soft
knuckle boy with question marks for teeth. you lunch table
magician spinning tales from thin air. the thing about
masks is someone always sees the string behind your head

•

you knew what was coming if you slept past 8 a.m. &
if it wasn't a cold bucket of water it would
have been the leather belt she kept soaking in the sink.
praise the mercy of your mother. praise the water that
awoke your still body from slumber. the sudden jolt
of relief in finding your drowning was just a dream
or, rather, just a moment. praise then, too, every soft
punishment: the gun-barrel stare, the one-leg-book-bal
ancing act in the corner, the rice cutting stars in
to your knees. praise the spatula & the upturned palm
the basement stairs & stale saltine crackers for dinner.
hosanna, the overgrown weeds & the tree switch that
refused to break. remember: this hurts her more than you

•

in class: when called on like a thief & something on you
stiffens, hardens & hangs like an ornament, like a
wooden plank & you must walk it to the front of the

room. your heart will become a drum, you will forget the
reason of your feet, your face will call your bluff, this is
the fifth time this week your body has become a bus
& swallowed you under it. there is no equation
for correcting an unwanted erection. walk with
hands hammered into the stitching of your pockets, pre
tend to be searching for the sun. set your binder be
fore your zipper & tap your thumb, play it cool, cock
your chin back, break no sweat. you soldier of study, you
bucket of brave, you Fruit of the Loom panic, got this!

•

possessed or bold, stealthy-like-hawk you steal a cigar
from your uncle's jacket. nevermind he just got out
of prison & has a circus wire temper. you've
seen the way smoke bellows from his blackened lips & think
you, too, can make smoke rise, front flip up your throat & slide
down your nostrils. puff out a ring to slide on any
girl's naked finger. too cool for school & too hot for
curfew, you stuff your pants with a sock & learn to walk
chest puffed & panting. learn to show your teeth & drool with
out reason. gasoline for ego. bloodtype: ticking
preteen is a shirt too small for your budding muscles
you take the tattered lighter found on your way home from
school. light. inhale & keep the smoke safely in your cheeks

•

neon green skinny jeans. frohawk dyed hot cheeto red
the New Boyz just released *Imma Jerk* & 7th grade bursts
into a carnival of cut up khakis, spiked glass
es, clorox bleached goodwill bought polo shirts. we glue
glitter on frazzled, handmade capris & dance as if
trying to escape the devil. craft death-defying
routines of knee-drops & gliding. spend recess choosing
teams & battling to music made with our mouths. gen
der doesn't exist when everyone wants to move their

hips, grind, prance. wobble & wear their sister's tight denims
you: the class conductor, the color queen of rhythm
with Kool-Aid in your hair are finally free. have found
a way to squeeze *faggotry* into a year-long fad

●

you don't clean to the same music you cook to. not
in this house, where everything is an antique & cloaked
in plastic. not when Janet's *I get so lonely* comes
on, the perfect tempo to scrub the black ring from the
porcelain tub & Luther is wailing about loss
when you got fresh collards cackling on the stove. you
don't cook while you clean unless you want a hint of
Pine-Sol in the peach cobbler. unless you enjoy the
roundabout task of making a mess after wiping
one up. this is my first lesson in first impressions:
bleach the countertop until it reflects the ceiling
fan, season the chicken until it glistens, set the
good plates, scrub like jesus christ is coming to dinner

●

somewhere they're sagging their pants & language into slang
they're resting their tongues in the mouths of a daughter, some
where a mother becomes a *bitch* by definition
of decedent. somewhere they're singing sin like gospel
hymns. somewhere a son is given a name & a gun
somewhere there is liquor licking a sister's breast. some
where there is smoke painting the breath of youth. somewhere
there is a white pill being placed in the punch bowl. some
where a sister is sneaking out an open window.
somewhere there is a brown boy, wrestling with the war
weeping in his chest, a blank page awaiting his breath.
somewhere there is a poem hiding in his heart, scattered
like glass, he is more beautiful when broken. somewhere

●

school: heat rakes skin raw & you find yourself lost in the
mirror, trying to make smooth the flaky flesh resting
on the dirt road of your reflection. your face: a pim
ple stained glass window wearing a million tiny pus filled rea
sons to leave. during lunch you bring bottles of chemi
cal cottage cheese to paint into the sidewalk of your
cheeks. learn words like *ugly, crater.* they creep into sca
bbing skin & stick like some sort of kick-me sign. cold wa
ter relaxes the skin, school bathroom tissue could be
mistook for cardboard but you use it anyway. learn
to pat, not wipe. hot water kills the germs, rinse your fin
gers, relearn words like love, it is the best adjective
for beauty. you were born without language for *perfect*

•

you can't come over unless you pass my mother's back
ground test. unless my mom spoke with your mom two months be
fore & planned to cook a meal together. unless your
mom makes you wash dishes with scalding water too. un
less your mom has checked for lice & don't mind Marvin Gaye
sobbing through the stereo. unless my mom knows if
your mom washes her greens before they touch the stove. un
less your shoes stay at the front door too. unless your grades
are better than mine. you can't come over unless it's
a weekend & your homework is checked. unless you brought
church clothes & a face towel. unless your mom voted for
Obama, both times. unless you know how to pull a
weed from the root. unless you know: *my mother don't play*

•

do you still perform autopsies on conversations
you've had lives ago? are you still wondering what gen
der the voice in your head is? is it still asking for
a name? because today you watched him. thought his voice cot
ton candy melting beneath your tongue. his hand: the best

piece of jewelry on the playground. today you don't
want your hands. think them too rough, too big for your wrists. bend
dangled. 8th grade & *god hates the gays*. you don't know words
like *spectrum, fluid*. weren't taught their taste, they too sweet &
mother never allowed her boys too much sugar. so
you shift. alter your taste at the altar. become some
thing worthy to call man. they'll build the closet for you
& spend the rest of their lives begging you to come out

•

night: when heat rakes skin raw & you become aroused at
the sound of thunder, your bed will beckon company
your palms, glowing pink, pulsing like the red bellies of
hungry wolves, will want to migrate south, between steaming
thighs. the fear of sin has settled, something here is grow
ing, your heart is sweating, your chest: a rising river
ready to release. your bed is rockin to the rhy
thm of you, your face wine red, drunk on steam & simul
ated sex, your body thrusting at the thought of him.
he is in your english class, wears his smile soft, his
touch a torch & you are sawdust, you a cotton sky
ready to rain, trembling like flood water. like salt
ed skin, like thunder. roar! rage! release, again. then sleep

•

*bro, i loved your poem, no homo. great job in gym to
day, no homo. do you know what's for lunch, no homo
can i borrow a pencil, no homo. nice hair cut
no homo. did you do the homework, no homo. are
those new shoes, no homo. you got a jump-shot, no ho
mo. can i copy your homework, no homo. what page
number we on, no homo. do you need a ride, no
homo. who you like, no homo. what class you got, no
homo. "kill, marry, or fuck," no homo. battle me
bro, no homo. you trying out for the play, no ho
mo. when can i come over, no homo. what answer*

you get, no homo. you know she like you right, no ho
mo. you should write a poem about me bro, no homo

•

13 & everything is a mirror: & you can't decide
what to wear. how to please everyone & still like what
you got on. your birthday two months away & mom can't
find her lipstick, thinks Aunt Charlotte took it. the same
summer Sherman tells you to take off your purple scarf
& you do & you laugh less because Uncle Paul say:
a smiling boy is a sweet boy. so you flex your
jaw & you watch your walk. become a weapon to pro
tect your sisters with. fourteen is a shirt too big for
your meager shoulders, your journals & private browsing.
fourteen ain't got no room for your pretty words or clean
nails. role models of mechanical tools give you a
hammer to become, so you throw yourself at the glass

she's dead : *you're dead*

she didn't suffer : *she is now suffering*

i love you : *i'll leave you*

she's dead : *the earth gets hungry too*

i'm sorry for your loss : *i can't afford this kind of grief right now*

i'm sorry for your loss : *if i had two bodies, i would loan you one*

i love you : *if you died it would affect me*

i'm sorry for your loss : *people die all the time*

i love you : *don't kill yourself*

i love you : *we can't afford another funeral*

she didn't suffer : *she didn't fight*

how are you : *your teeth are growing beige*

how's your semester : *i can smell your grief*

are you still living on campus : *how much time are you spending alone*

can i hug you : *you still have your body*

she's dead : *you still have classwork to do*

she's dead : *does that mean you pay me back*

my _____ died last year : *people die all the time*

my deepest condolences : *if you died i would make a Facebook status*

you're in my thoughts & prayers : *thank God it wasn't me*

i feel your pain : *i, too, can cry*

i am here for you : *i will like every status you post*

she will be missed : *i haven't talked to her in twenty years*

i love you : *shcszshcszshcszshcszshszshszshschsz*

i love you : *82%ofteensuicidesaresuccessfulwithagun*

i love you : *...i don't know what's up there beyond the sky...*

she didn't suffer : *didn't she want to be cremated?*

she didn't suffer : *your mother never liked crowded places...*

she didn't suffer : *don't you know a wooden casket can take centuries to rot*

OLD RONDO - AGE 16
for Irene and Mom and those removed

we were ferris wheel watchers. firefly fighters. dollar store cap gun robbers—cops & Sunday-creased collars. private school scholars (giving the church basket the dollars our mothers slipped into our pockets seconds before) we held doors for our elders & snuck to receive communion even though our tongues hadn't reached their stage of holy. water guns weren't allowed in our homes

but balloons were so we soaked our summers in battleship. bottled water sipped through naive nine-year-old lips. horizon sunset sitting on jj hill. waiting for those street lamps to call us home before our mothers did & when she slept, we ditched our screen doors. danced in rain. rinsed out our grass stains & became the night's nickname. they called us kids

we called ourselves bigger than most things our size. sneaking girls beneath the playground slide. first kisses were a lot like gut laughter everything was funnier when you weren't supposed to smile. they told us to mind our manners. fold our fingers. *did you wash your hands before dishing them greens? did you help your mother pick them greens?* we were scabbed knees & bubble gum fiends all hyped up on Mike & Ikes and Now & Laters

"eat some now, & save some for later" sounded a lot like a metaphor for childhood. for the way we grew up through adversity & anniversaries of street signs & jazz parades. i guess, before they built that freeway, there was a colony of houses. lined up like heritage on an auction block about to meet their god. the largest black community in Saint Paul was cut down. like it hadn't deserved the land it slept on for so long. like it hadn't raised its children under corner store stories, front porches & grandma's front lawn

i bet if they knew we hid beneath the bridges they built they would tear those down too. they would tell us kids to grow up like high rises through minority roofs. we were minorities, proof—that if you raise your fireflies in the heart of the dark, they will earn their light in the form of a spark! in the form of a million matches attempting to set aflame the desert until every grain is a diamond worth giving a name. so they called us kids. we called ourselves the reason this neighborhood lives we were our front door keys. our tattered shoes & collard greens. our mothers woke us at dawn. told us to walk down the block to Golden Thyme given enough money for a coffee & a Krispy Kreme. if i remember to bring four creams, four sugars a stir. she would always blow me a wink. one that meant the top of the world, or at least, the ferris wheel peak.

WHAT THE DEAD KNOW BY HEART

lately, when asked *how are you,* i
respond with a name no longer living

Rekia, Jamar, Sandra, Philando

i am alive by luck at this point. i wonder
often: if the gun that will unmake me
is yet made, what white birth

will bury me, how many bullets, like a
flock of blue jays, will come carry my black
to its final bed, which photo will be used

to water down my blood. today i did
not die & there is no god or law to
thank. the bullet missed my head

& landed in another. today, i passed
a mirror & did not see a body, instead
a suggestion, a debate, a blank

post-it note there looking back. i
haven't enough room to both rage and
weep. i go to cry & each tear turns
to steam. I say

I matter & a ghost
white hand appears
over my mouth

THE ORPHAN PERFORMS AN AUTOPSY ON OLD RONDO - AGE 20

for those who continue to be removed

we   watch   fire   guns.
      cops   crease
                      our mothers.
        we held   our elders.
even   our tongues.   guns
      allowed

              nine-year-old   s   on to set.
waiting for   streets   to call   others.
                            rain rinsed
        the night.

   call   ourselves bigger   beneath
the   ground   *gut*   *everything*
       you weren't supposed to   *mind.*

                  Mike

                 sounded a lot like

        jazz   before   there
was   an auction block   to
                        cut
       the
child.   store   front   and   fire.

  heart   in the form of
      match   flame   until every
                   kid
        lives.

    our   tattered
mothers awoke   the block to

            stir
      the world

WHITENESS SHOPS FOR A PRAYER

how do you pray / does it involve a keyboard / is it in 140 characters / or less /
does it have a barcode / does it have a Wikipedia page / is it in English / is it tax
deductible / does it include all lives / is your prayer gluten free / is it safe around
children / is there an abridged version / is your prayer an all purpose cleaner / nat-
ural selection / can it get out the black / can it clean up the tough stains / is your
prayer running for president / can your prayer run / does it do yoga / is it active / i
don't understand can you translate / can you teach me / can your prayer teach / is
it articulate / where can i get one / where is it from / is it in right now / is it spicy
/ will it burn my tongue / does it come with anything else / compound interest /
buy one get one free / is it exclusive / can i join / do i have to close my eyes / or can
i just post it / does it hang well / polyester / silk / is it safe online / does it have a
Facebook option / paris filter / does it love its country / it has to love its country /
was it born here / is it pre-washed / will it attack: my opinion / does it come / with
a leash / how much / is it reusable / which religion / can i crop it / one size fits /
all / where was it made / can you prove it / is it carbonated / is it domestic / is it
domesticated / is it sharp / is it natural / where is it from / does your prayer have
papers / does it come with instructions / how does it look / does it bite / how does
it look / does it fit / how does it look / how does it look / how does it look / does
it come / in white

THE ORPHAN PERFORMS AN AUTOPSY ON THE NATIONAL ANTHEM

you

proud.   we

fight.
we

red
bursting in
the night.
our flag was

the land.

NEW COUNTRY

after Safia Elhillo

i pledge allegiance to my
mother's garden & leftover
greens & lawry's seasoning
salt & cast-iron skillets hung
like new rusting crucifixes
beside the stove

i pledge allegiance to Solange &
coconut oil   i pledge allegiance
to grindr & my nudes sent like shiny
brown flags   i pledge allegiance to
the inside joke & Black Twitter   to
selby ave   the side eye emoji   free
open mics & to laughter breaking
like bread

yeah i'm salty af   that's what
happens when you're dragged across
an ocean   when you're curved by a
country that soaks its feet in your blood
i pledge allegiance to no bullet or ballad
no they or bald bird or well-intentioned
white women offering hugs

i choose the cypher at dusk   the
swaying circle & the music we make
with our mouths   our good mouths
& the ghosts that sometimes crawl out
i choose *Sunday Candy's* chorus   our
humming bodies & the street lamp
flickering on

beat   this impromptu preamble
warmed by our own   resilience i

choose the bus stop   & the soft whir
of dead leaves   november's falling sun
good soft light   stretching our dancing
shadows   tossing us into the night's cool air

THE ORPHAN DINES WITH GHOSTS

there are dead boys   at the dinner table
& white women running   out of words   to compliment the turkey

they say *soft*
        & i imagine the salt & smack of a bullet
        rattling like a pinball in a black boy's jaw

they say *more pepper*
        & my melanin remembers how sugar is a spice
        to an open wound then begins to melt

they say *too dry*
        & Ferguson & Minneapolis & Detroit &&&
        become a death desert; a bouquet of wilting
        girls left to give the ground some color

they say *stuffed*
        & wilson's bank account becomes flooded
        with ancient blood, begins to pay bills with
        a dead boy's bones

they say *so good*
        & all the ghosts resurrect. begin to suck their teeth
        to blow on the back of pale necks

Donte, why haven't you touched your food? Why so quiet? Donte, why so quiet?

because we're being   hunted.   always. bound
like wheat left to soil under sun   & you sit sighing   about your privilege. full stomach
foreign to the bodies you break   bread over. got crumbs nested   in my brother's
corpse & i'm pissed.   have justified our murders too.   dissected the lettering of my
autopsy   in search of any hiding justice   somewhere living   is a man
paid to make our mothers mourn.   somewhere living is a law that says my brothers &
i can't walk   three or more in North Minneapolis.   somewhere living is white
america. laughing. licking spoons in their living room   unbothered.   breathing. the news
cheerleading their silence.   historically violent headlines: *looting after innocent verdict*
& you ma'am   want me to be quiet   want me black enough   for decoration.

want me two words or less.   obituary ready & dressed. *boy just dance off those bullets, just write*
a poem about progression. want me articulate   until the trigger. won't understand racism
until someone calls me   a n/i/g/g/e/r   until then, you won't riot. & we'll
just sit.   cutlery awkwardly cutting the silence   culturally divided

you'll say   *something about this meal is off*

& i'll think

 white guilt must make
 everything taste like
 a grave

IN WHICH THE ORPHAN'S SISTER IS MURDERED SIX MONTHS AFTER HIS MOTHER'S DEATH

it wasn't bad enough that she was shot in front of her children
  her body lay six hours in the July rain
  the news report said: *female* & not *woman*
  the whole neighborhood watched   but no one saw a thing
  she wasn't the *intended target*
  she warmed a plate for a man who would, eventually, use her as a shield
  i ran from 5th & Penn, pajamas only, wailing harder than the sky
  someone stole gifts from the tree-curb memorial
  her daughters whispered *get up, get up* at the casket
  she registered to return to school in the fall
  she cried the first time she fired a gun
  mom dreamt she would be the first of us to go

i could let the blood return to my molting brain, unpin revenge
from its crowded shrine where i've planned to toss his crimson
body one splashing limb at a time. i could, so easily, let my heart
back inside this burning house. return the shovels to my mother's forgotten
shed, unlearn the recipe for hydrochloric acid. i could forfeit the
hunt, i promise. i am a kind boy. just don't tell me that

  she bought him a bullet-proof vest
  she died in his arms
  he dropped her spilling body & fled

FIVE STAGES OF GRIEF

denial

my mother is dead
mother is dead my
is dead my mother
dead my mother is

dead my is mother
is dead mother my
mother is my dead
my mother dead is

dead is my mother
my dead mother is
mother my is dead
is mother dead my

is mother my dead
mother my dead is
my dead is mother
dead is mother my

dead mother my is
mother dead is my
my is mother dead
is mother dead my

my is dead mother
is my dead mother
mother dead my is
is my mother dead

anger

& i wish there was a soft metaphor
to lower you into this grief. instead

i will say *i didn't kill myself because
i knew my siblings couldn't afford
another funeral.* i will say *each night
i dreamt of stealing back her body*
not a hooked rope naively thrown toward heaven
not a bandit thieving god's house of what belongs
to me. i mean, i grabbed a shovel. i mean, she's buried
on dale & larpenteur & taught all of her children how
best to tend stubborn dirt

bargaining

i had wanted nothing more than to survive my childhood.
to walk clean-faced and unfrayed out of that constant alarm.
to mourn her is to mourn the belt & the hands that held the belt
& the heart that held the hands that spilled my blood like juice
across the kitchen linoleum

don't use my good towels either

besides, what good is survival's trophy if your assailant is dead?
come back. even if it means your hug is a hand around my throat
even if your kiss is delivered with a fist. o' how quickly i would
crawl back into that haunted house, that graveyard where every
hymn goes to die. o how ready i am to be thinned with fear, seven
& tear-drunk. to heave & pop like ready oil. to throw a knife at
the family portrait. to soar *b::::h* from my lips like a fevered bird.
to wish her dead beneath my breath while i scrub myself off the floor

rakes the night sky of its stars, keeps them as leverage, as bulb-less lamps in the basement of me. i am alive if alive means to be a moth caught in the hands of some childish grief. shake me to see if i am still breathing. burn my wings if i'm not

confession: the want to die is not always the want not to live, but sometimes the want to live somewhere softer. where the tall grass lulls my body to sleep where everything promises to stay alive

acceptance

GRIEF, AGAIN

every black woman with grey hair is your dead mother you collapse in Walmart knees buckled at the sight of an electric scooter you wrap yourself around yourself & wail into a naked mattress your lover's hand is placed like heated stones along your heaving back you don't want to be touched & want to be touched everywhere you show the dean the death certificate & are allowed to stay another semester drowning would be easiest you think as rain draws razor thin lines down your bedroom window grief is a paper cut at every bend in your body grief shaves each bone down to a shriveled white flag you want to die but don't want to leave a mess you throw a mug across the kitchen & envy its sudden dissection every word your mother last spoke scuttles like mice in your deserted head memory is a ruptured organ memory is a ghost begging for new flesh memory taps a gun to your inner skull & demands you bring back the dead

TEETHING: A CRUMBLING PANTOUM

In my worst dream all of my teeth fall out
    I awake like a fire choking on air
    Teeth are the hardest substance in the human body
    Suddenly, I am the boy defined by what he has lost

I awake as a fire choking on air & the mother
    sharpens my name with her tongue, whittles it down
    to *faggot*. Suddenly, I am the boy defined by what is given to him
    What is a dream / if not the mind pulling ribbons from my throat

The mother sharpens my skin with *faggot*, whittles me down
    with Leviticus. The uncle says *one gay nephew has flooded*
    enough. What are teeth / if not the telling of which parts
    of you most easily soften when sweet

To be queer & black is to walk out of the closet
    into a casket. My queer says my black has flooded enough
    The mother says *confession, says communion, drink the blood*
    says to be straight, to be calm, to pray, to kneel eager with a ready
    mouth before god

    & what is left to do

    but pluck the bones

    from my face

ALPHABET SOUP

say: f a t h e r

& each letter will become
a bird fleeing my mind's

nest. ask where & the *f*
will curl itself beneath my

mother's chin. waiting for
grief, that chewed & still

kicking worm to drop into
its ready mouth. ask of the

divorce & the *a* hurls itself
into every window of that

house. each thump, a cracked
& unanswered neck carpeting

the lawn. *divorce.* how pretty
a name for such a sloppy

wreckage & maybe it was a
slow decision, one letter collected

for every new child he found
my mother nursing in the kitchen

didn't like all of the stray cribs
crowding the entry. must have

curled his lips as she offered
adoption? as she would leftover

soup, a second option when all
the good meat has gone sour

when the good, woman body
is said spoiled for what it can

not produce. when a black woman
body is not a body but now, a napkin

he uses to wipe his mouth   full of
what my mother's hands have made

THE ORPHAN PERFORMS AN AUTOPSY ON ADOPTION

you ask	for a beginning, i speak to you
of a ship	sailing my blood, there was a continent
mistook	for a country
mistook	for a cake & then
a feast.	ghost white hands licking brown frosting from their fingers.
auction.	swelter. fade to black. & then my birth:
a red ocean	coughs up a kicking boy & then the ocean recedes.
you ask	for *more specific biology*, i speak of
wind.	of invisible blood, moonlit flight, of a boy floating from
hospital	to foster home until, finally, a woman picks the boy made entirely
of sand.	until finally she teaches him to spell his tired name,
you ask	for a name,
you ask	for an I.D, a certificate, a photo
you ask	& ask & ask

listen, once, i said *adopted* & the class fainted
with laughter. once, i called a stranger my father
because the lunch table began to grow teeth. i know

i have a body, it is solid. i have a navel like an x on a map.
easy evidence of some lost country, some removed mother,
unearthed grief. a voyage away from that song-drunk land.

adoption: the most beautiful erasure, the most successful
punchline. a lineage snapped at the neck then nursed back to
flight. look at the boy with water for blood. look at the boy

twice removed from his identity. do not ask me if i know
whose body i belong to. do not ask me which are my real
siblings. if blood is thicker than water then love must be

thicker than both. must be some new soft country, some damp
fertile dirt. perhaps i was born & then born again. perhaps
i am here without a language, without a lantern to lead me home.

but look at the moon making sugar of its light & look at each
hair of grass naming themselves. & sure, i am here like a gust
of wind, the luck of some slow erosion

sure, i exist   like everything's busy child
like a handprint   left in the sand

ALTERNATE BEGINNING: THE GAME

is simple & played with my brother
in the backseat, as each home flutters
past you point & say *yes* or *no*

yes, you would live there
no, you would not

maybe a home
with grass, the good kind, the shiny kind, the kind outside
the courthouse. the kind that reaches all the way to the curb:
no dirt patches, no dead bulking brown, no yellow weeded
intruders spotting through crumbling cement, no abandoned
sideways tricycle, rain rusted & waiting & waiting

maybe a home
with a tree fit for five-year-old feet, a garden even, visible
from the street. maybe our newer mother will grow things.
good things. the nutritious kind. the kind that chemicals cannot
produce. the kind that doesn't kindle or make lamar, my older
bro, cough like he does. like a factory in his chest or a fight

maybe a home
with windows, ones you can see both in & out of, & curtains
blue & wavy, then sometimes it'll be like you're near the water
& river weed & sleep will come easy. unlike breath, unlike
those men with badges on their chests always upturning the mattress
dumping out cabinets, like they searching for something bad
something they need, something bagged & that easily burns

maybe a home
with brick or blue plaster with ribbons tied to the railing, maybe
they'll know we're coming, maybe they won't know where we've been
then it'll be like we're new & nameless. a porch swing. a welcome
mat. *yes, yes*

i ask the man driving if adoption hurts like a needle. i ask if lamar,
my older bro will be there too. to him my questions are caught flies
charging the glass. he opens the window & out falls my: *yes, yes*

                                        maybe a home
                        with a porchlight. maybe a home
                        with a white fence. maybe a home
                            without holes. maybe a home
                    with fresh pain   t. maybe a home
                    without screams in the front screens
                            yes, yes. maybe a home
                        with a doorbell. maybe a home
                                        with a door

ADOPTION DAY: HOMECOMING, 1998

for Lamar

if to die means to dream forever, to live among the shapeless & hovering
i know what story keeps my mother company. if you knew her you knew
about the dream, the one where her fruitless body wished for the plum
skinned boy & then the boy walks through her front door. if you did
not know her, here:

Characters:
>   Aunt Paula
>   Aunt Nancy
>   Aunt Charlotte

*it was like she saw a ghost | mmm-mm | just like that | a ghost | jumped up &
er' thang | damn near jumped out her skin | mmm-mm | hollering 'bout some
dream | just like Mary ain't it, dreaming of ghosts | just like her | mmm-mm |
damn near scared the children | damn near made the social worker send y'all back
| hollering like she was | said she seen him before | your brother | dreamt up his
bones | said she labored him every night for nine months | every night | she said
| crying like she be | just like Mary ain't it, always crying | all: always | took his
face between her palms | real tight | like she was praying | like his face was the
New Testament | weeping like she was | & she was | examining his face like fruit
| looking for a bruise | some birthmark | some evidence only she could under-
stand | your mother child | child, your momma | boy your mother must have
found it | must have seen what she was looking for | all: must have fell in love |
must have wept the Red Sea | & that's when she jumped |she did | flame like |
screaming like she was | it's him! | kept saying, it's him! | her tears drawing lines
on his face | his face wide eyed & puffy | his face a fruit rinsed clean | held him
close | held you too | breathless & sweatin' like she just gave birth | like y'all was
blood | or panting & covered in hers | you was there | don't you remember | was
nothin' but two years old | couldn't have | all: mm-mmmm | your momma was |
boy your mom | child, your mother was | all: somethin' else*

i don't remember this bloodless birth. our second mother holding our small bod-
ies to her breast. but i know it happened. i've seen the photos. i've met strangers
who, i hear, took turns carrying me on their shoulders. and i will not beg for you

to believe this gentle miracle, this impossible bedtime story shared whenever we needed a reminder of who we belonged to. how strange now that she is gone & we are the ones rushing home to sleep. hoping to lay down our grief. hoping, if only for a moment, she appears, laughing in our dreams.

TO KEEP FROM SAYING ORPHAN

adopted
if i say it fast enough
it sounds like *i—a—m—dead*

iamadopted/iamadopted/iamadopted

which means it could be   worse
which means my life is
only valuable compared to   worse

it does this, my head i mean. makes
every poem a beatless body. which

makes my mouth a morgue. which
makes my mouth a catharsis of ash

which makes you a witness to this
wilting. which means sometimes i
stay up & rehearse

my own going. i practice the release
of my own ghost into the night. each
poem eulogizing

a limb or
an organ or
a thought

each poem some mortician's headache
each poem badly embalmed: missing
teeth

which makes my mouth a closed casket
which means i mourn in metaphor
which means my parent(s)

could be the shovel
or the dirt or the tree
owl interrogating the night

do you hear them asking

who
who, took
my boy?

GRIEF SESTINA

you've heard *grief turns the body to stone*
like some brash & greedy lover, the earth
curls its frigid limbs around your mother's
body. death is the only possible thing
she would put before her children's
needs & you need so badly for winter

to release its grip, reverse each winter
flake resting too boldly on her tombstone.
an absence so thick, her eleven children
begin to erase. begin to envy the earth
for its ability to hunger—to call anything
food. this is the first funeral your mother

will not sing you through. grief mothers
your tuneless bones. January holds winter
like a sobbing brother while everything
reminds you of what final seed or stone
your body will become to fertilize the earth.
who are you, now, if not your mother's child?

orphan means you are everything's child
or orphan means the land is your mother
or orphan means you belong to the earth
even when, like a groggy, silent god, winter
comes to sharpen every song to stone.
you've heard *death is natural* then everything

come spring, must grieve. to thaw is a thing
of release. of new, wet life beckoning a child's
hands. look at how mud can clean any stone
in the garden. carefully make out your mother's
face among the good soil. yes donte, winter
will leave & will come again & from the earth

will grow her smile flagging in April's earthly
wind. a bulb. a stem. a stalk braving anything
threatening sunlight. yes donte, winter
will leave & will take her body with. children
stand & sing: *sometimes I feel like a motherless*
& the church joins *motherless child.* stone

tongues singing to stone: *sometimes i feel* earth
becoming *motherless.* you are everything's
sweet *child,* singing in hopes to melt winter

LONG STORY SHORT

after Mary Lou Collins

someone who is dead now taught you
how best to clean up your blood. then
how to clean up blood when it is not
your own. how to push from your elbow
properly sweep a floor, spell c o n t i n u e

three syllables donte, go on & like a god
or a bird, or a boy salted with grief, you
want the earth to kneel for you, want every
clock to confess its slick motive. to say,
suddenly, that death is only a joke

the earth's biggest punchline. she's been
gone 15,840 minutes & you have felt the
godless storm of each of them, are waiting
for your mother to walk into her funeral, to
sit next to all of her children at once, to lean
into the soft of her shoulder, for her to whisper
it's okay son, i'm here now, i'm here

ACKNOWLEDGEMENTS

Thank you to the editors of these journals, where some of these poems previously appeared:

The Academy of American Poets: "What the Dead Know by Heart"
Vinyl Poetry and Prose: "Grief, Again," "Whiteness Shops for a Prayer,"
    and "Sonnet on Sweet"
The Saint Paul Almanac: "Old Rondo"

For my siblings, each of you. Destiny, your journals gifted me new lan- guage as a child, sorry for invading your privacy. Karl, Tomica, Eric, Ty, A.J.—your patience was necessary. Lamar, Antonio, Antoine—thank you for listening to my rough drafts. Tamiea, Keiony—welcome to the family. Crystal, I hope you're dancing with Mom; I love you.

For my community, my TruArtSpeaks family—where would I be without your honesty and friendship? Chava, Tamera, Laresa, Lucien, Duncan, Julie, Armand, Ramaj, Tequa—the best teammates I could ask for. Fatima, thank you for making time for my sadness. My mentors—Adam, Khary, Danez, Kyle, Desdemona, your courage inspires mine. Tish Jones—for investing in my teenage angst, for asking me *What do you care about? Who are you?*

Sarah Ogutu—you understand the methods to my madness. Blythe, Erica, Sam, Sierra, Hieu—thank you for letting me be extra. Sarah Myers—for actively listen-ing. For my teachers, your encouragement led me here— Courtney, Emily, Kevin, Shaun, Amy, the Zosels, the Fiegis.

For those living and deceased who continue to inspire my work. For those who hold me accountable, who let me be human. For my mother, my favorite poet.

ABOUT THE AUTHOR

Donte is a 21-year-old queer, black poet whose first poem was written at the age of seven about feeling trapped, unheard. Named the first Youth Poet Laureate of Saint Paul, Minnesota, they are the author of *Autopsy* (Button Poetry) and winner of the 2016 Most Promising Young Poet Award from the Academy of American Poets. Collins is the recipient of the 2016 Mitchell Prize in Poetry and is currently a junior at Augsburg College. They are an alum of TruArtSpeaks, a non-profit arts organization based out of the Twin Cities cultivating literacy, leadership and social justice through the study & application of Hip Hop culture, as well as a current board member of Black Table Arts.

Cave Canem founder Toi Derricotte featured Donte in the Academy of American Poets, calling their work "sophisticated and emotionally mature". Donte's words cannot sit still and often embody theatrical recitations. Their work holds a knife to systems of oppression and dominant power structures. They wield poetry to collapse normativity and deliver work that is both alluring and challenging. Often centered around intersections of class, race, adoption, sexuality and social justice, Donte uses pause, rhythm, raw fierce emotion, and the marriage between archive and repertoire to reimagine how poetry can be accessible to those who believe the form is dead. National Book Critics Circle Award Recipient Claudia Rankine shared a poem by Donte at the 2016 Dodge Poetry Festival. Donte resides in Saint Paul, Minnesota, where they hibernate during the winter and seriously consider purchasing a warmer yet less fashionable jacket.

OTHER BOOKS BY BUTTON POETRY

If you enjoyed this book, please consider checking out some of our others, below. Readers like you allow us to keep broadcasting and publishing. Thank you!

Sam Sax, *A Guide to Undressing Your Monsters*

Mahogany L. Browne, *smudge*

Neil Hilborn, *Our Numbered Days*

Sierra DeMulder, *We Slept Here*

Danez Smith, *black movie*

Cameron Awkward-Rich, *Transit*

Jacqui Germain, *When the Ghosts Come Ashore*

Hanif Willis-Abdurraqib, *The Crown Ain't Worth Much*

Aaron Coleman, *St. Trigger*

Olivia Gatwood, *New American Best Friend*

Melissa Lozada-Oliva, *peluda*

William Evans, *Still Can't Do My Daughter's Hair*

Rudy Francisco, *Helium*

Sabrina Benaim, *Depression & Other Magic Tricks*

Available at buttonpoetry.com/shop and more!